Contents

Welcome to Spain!

Hello! My name's Benjamin Blog and this is Barko Polo, my **inquisitive** dog. (He's named after ancient ace explorer **Marco Polo**.) We have just got back from our latest adventure – exploring Spain. We put this book together from some of the blog posts we wrote on the way.

N

Bay of Biscay

FRANCE

ANDORRA

Bilbao

Pyrenees Mountains

River Ebro

River Duero

Barcelona

ntic
ean

Menorca

Madrid

PORTUGAL

River Tagus

SPAIN

Mallorca

River Guadiana

Valencia

Balearic Islands

Ibiza

Formentera

River Guadalquivir

Mar Menor

Seville

Mediterranean
Sea

Málaga

Gibraltar (British)

Ceuta (Spanish)

——— Country borders

Melilla
(Spanish)

ALGERIA

MOROCCO

BARKO'S BLOG-TASTIC SPAIN FACTS

Spain is a country in the south-west of Europe. It is part of a **peninsula** that sticks out into the Atlantic Ocean. On land, it has borders with Portugal, France, Gibraltar and Andorra.

The story of Spain

Posted by: Ben Blog | 6 March at 10.03 a.m.

We are here at the Altamira Cave in northern Spain on the first stop of our tour. I wanted to see the famous cave paintings that were made by **prehistoric** people thousands of years ago. You can't go inside the original cave, but a **replica** has been built next door. Look at that **bison**!

In the 15th and 16th centuries, many explorers set out from Spain to find new **trade routes** around the world. One of the most famous was Cristóbal Colón. He is now known as Christopher Columbus.

Mountains, islands, rivers and parks

Posted by: Ben Blog | 19 April at 2.21 p.m.

Our next stop was the Pyrenees, a mountain range that lies along the border with France. It stretches for about 430 kilometres (270 miles) and is a brilliant place to explore. We're off to climb Pico de Aneto, the highest peak in the Pyrenees. See you in around 12 hours!

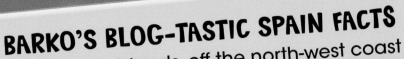

BARKO'S BLOG-TASTIC SPAIN FACTS

The Canary Islands, off the north-west coast of Africa, are part of Spain. There are seven islands in the chain. The biggest is Tenerife, home to Pico de Teide, which is a huge, **active volcano**.

From the Pyrenees, we headed a short way south to Zaragoza. The city stands on the Ebro, the longest river in Spain. The Ebro flows for 910 kilometres (565 miles) from the mountains in Cantabria into the Mediterranean Sea. I'm standing on the Puente de Piedra bridge across the river.

BARKO'S BLOG-TASTIC SPAIN FACTS

Doñana National Park is an area of marshes, streams and sand dunes in southern Spain. Here, the River Guadalquivir flows into the sea. The National Park is home to the very rare Iberian lynx.

Spanish cities

Today, we headed to Madrid, the capital city of Spain. Barko took this snap of me at the Royal Palace. The Royal Family of Spain lives here. This is one of the biggest palaces in Europe. It has more than 3,000 rooms! We're about to set off on a tour – I hope we don't get lost.

BARKO'S BLOG-TASTIC SPAIN FACTS

The city of Barcelona is packed with amazing buildings. This is the Sagrada Família. It is a huge church, designed by the **architect** Antoni Gaudí. It has never been finished!

Buenos días!

Most Spanish people speak Spanish. Spanish is also spoken by millions of people around the world. I've been trying to learn a few words. *Buenos días!* means "Good day", but you can also say *Hola!* ("Hello"). *Por favor* is "please" and *gracias* is "thank you".

BARKO'S BLOG-TASTIC SPAIN FACTS

Family life is very important in Spain. People sometimes move away from their families to find work, but they like to get together in their spare time and help to look after each other.

15

It is **9.00 a.m.** and these Spanish children are starting school. For some children, the school day finishes at **2.00 p.m.** In summer, pupils have a long holiday that lasts from June until September. They have shorter breaks at Christmas and Easter.

BARKO'S BLOG-TASTIC SPAIN FACTS

In Andalucía in southern Spain, "white towns", like this one, are dotted about on the hills. All of the houses have **whitewashed** walls and get a fresh coat of paint every year.

Many Spanish people are **Roman Catholics**, and there are beautiful churches all around Spain. We've arrived in Santiago de Compostela. People come here from around the world to visit the cathedral. Some of them walk long distances to get here, as a sign of their faith.

BARKO'S BLOG-TASTIC SPAIN FACTS

Every year, in August, a very messy festival takes place in the town of Buñol. It is called La Tomatina. Thousands of people line the streets and throw tomatoes at each other for fun.

Feeling hungry

Posted by: Ben Blog | 15 November at 1.06 p.m.

For lunch today, we decided to try paella, a famous Spanish dish. It is made with rice, mixed with **seafood**, meat, tomatoes, peppers and saffron. It was so tasty that I had seconds! I'm looking forward to a siesta – a short nap you take after lunch.

BARKO'S BLOG-TASTIC SPAIN FACTS

Savoury snacks called tapas are very popular all over Spain. You can tuck into *patatas bravas* (spicy potatoes), tortilla (Spanish omelette), chorizo (spicy sausage), olives or juicy prawns, like these. Yum!

Sport and leisure

Posted by: Ben Blog | 29 December at 3.12 p.m.

Back in Madrid, we're at the Bernabéu Stadium to watch a football match. Real Madrid are playing. They are one of the top Spanish teams. Football is the most popular sport in Spain, and the fans here really get behind their team. *Hala*, Madrid! (Go, Madrid!)

BARKO'S BLOG-TASTIC SPAIN FACTS

Pelota is a Spanish ball game, played by two teams on a walled court. The players hit the ball with their hands or with wooden bats or baskets. The aim is to put the ball out of the other team's reach.

From tomatoes to tourism

Posted by: Ben Blog | 3 February at 2.56 p.m.

We're in Almeria, in southern Spain, visiting a tomato farm. Here, tomatoes, melons and peppers are grown in plastic greenhouses and sold all over Europe. Spanish farmers also grow crops such as oranges, mandarins, olives, almonds and grapes, for making wine.

BARKO'S BLOG-TASTIC SPAIN FACTS

Tourism is very important in Spain and earns lots of money for the country. Millions of holiday-makers visit Spain each year to enjoy the sunny weather and beautiful beaches.

And finally...

It's our last day and we have come to the Alhambra Palace in Granada. It was built in the 13th to 14th centuries by a **Moorish** king. I took this snap in the Court of the Lions. The fountain is held up by 12 white marble lions. Water spurts from the lions' mouths.

BARKO'S BLOG-TASTIC SPAIN FACTS

The Guggenheim in Bilbao is a spectacular museum. The building is covered in gleaming glass, **titanium** and **limestone**. Inside, there are exhibitions by famous artists and sculptors.

Spain fact file

Area: 505,370 square kilometres
(195,124 square miles)

Population: 46,704,314 (2013)

Capital city: Madrid

Other main cities: Barcelona, Valencia, Seville

Languages: Spanish (Castilian), Catalan,
Gallego, Euskera (Basque)

Main religion: Christianity (**Roman Catholic**)

Highest mountain: Pico de Teide
(3,718 metres/12,198 feet)

Longest river: Ebro (910 kilometres/565 miles)

Currency: Euro

Spain quiz

Find out how much you know about Spain with our quick quiz.

1. Which mountains lie between Spain and France?
a) Alps
b) Pyrenees
c) Rock of Gibraltar

2. Which is the longest river in Spain?
a) Ebro
b) Tagus
c) Guadalquivir

3. How do you say "thank you" in Spanish?
a) *Por favor*
b) *Hola*
c) *Gracias*

4. What is tapas?
a) a type of meal
b) a type of dancing
c) a type of fish

5. What is this?

Answers

1. b
2. a
3. c
4. a
5. Guggenheim, Bilbao

Glossary

active volcano volcano that is still erupting

architect person who designs buildings

bison large, bull-like animal with a huge head, shaggy hair and a humped back

inquisitive interested in learning about the world

limestone hard rock used as a building material

Marco Polo explorer who lived from about 1254 to 1324. He travelled from Italy to China.

Moorish relating to the Moors, Muslims who ruled parts of Spain during medieval times

peninsula thin strip of land that sticks out into the sea

prehistoric from a time long ago, before things were written down

replica exact copy of something

Roman Catholic Christian who belongs to the Roman Catholic Church

seafood food from the sea, such as prawns, squid and lobster

titanium strong, white metallic material

trade routes sea journeys taken by sailing ships to buy and sell goods in other countries

whitewashed painted with white paint

Find out more

Books

Spain (Been There), Annabel Savery (Wayland, 2011)

Spain (Countries Around the World), Charlotte Guillain (Raintree, 2012)

Spain (Countries in Our World), Sean Ryan (Franklin Watts, 2012)

Spain (Unpacked), Susie Brooks (Wayland, 2013)

Websites

ngkids.co.uk
National Geographic's website has lots of information, photos and maps of countries around the world.

www.worldatlas.com
Packed with information about different countries, this website has flags, time zones, facts and figures, maps and timelines.

Index